The Meaningful Trainer

Facilitating transformation in today's workplace

Kate Domenick, Ed. D.

David A. Gallup, Ed. D.

DEDICATION

To all the trainers who shared their stories with us—
thank you all!

CONTENTS

Introduction..i

1. Becoming a Meaningful Trainer....................................... 1

2. Preparing and Supporting Trainers 13

3. The Value of Reflection 31

4. The Meaningful Trainer and the Continuous
   Improvement Process 43

5. The Meaningful Trainer as a Role Model for the
   Organization..63

6. What It Means to be a Meaningful Trainer 69

Conclusion: Key Point Summary..73

Appendices:

    Trainer Survey 77

    Measuring Training Effectiveness Sample.................... 83

    Overview of Training Measurement: The 5 Levels......87

ACKNOWLEDGMENTS

The authors thank our two thoughtful reviewers for their help with the manuscript. Dick Sands and Kevin Brown are truly meaningful trainers who have served as an inspiration to many in the field. Dick and Kevin, the book owes much to both of you and we are most grateful for your help.

INTRODUCTION

Why We Train

Trainers train to make a difference—a difference to their trainees, to their organizations, and even to the larger community. Ask trainers why they do what they do and you're likely to hear something like this: "I get a kick out of helping people learn," or "I love seeing that a-ha moment in trainees."

No matter what subject trainers train—equipment operation, management skills, sales, good manufacturing practices—trainers are likely to value the experience of inspiring learners as much or even more than they value the

At the heart of being a meaningful trainer is the recognition that no enterprise can thrive if its employees do not grow – both in themselves and in their jobs.

subject they're training. In fact, in our hundreds of interviews and in formal studies of trainers, no trainer has ever told us she wants only to meet program objectives. That doesn't mean trainers don't care about meeting objectives—they do. But their job satisfaction is derived largely from their interaction with and impact on their trainees. It's personal to them.

Not surprisingly, many organizations tend to minimize the human element of training and focus instead on its more tangible aspects: behavioral objectives, performance outcomes, test results, business impact. Each of these is critical to the training effort, yet they are not necessarily the aspects of training that trainers in their heart of hearts value most. Trainers acknowledge that things like business impact are important, but they get their personal reward from helping learners learn.

The Human Side of Training

Trainers are agents of change, and as such they encounter all the obstacles and rewards associated with any attempt to challenge or modify the deeply held beliefs and age-old practices of a group. This is true even in—or especially in—competency-based training, where emotional elements are likely to intrude into the process despite the best efforts of program designers to remove subjectivity from the training. Validated lesson plans, objective tests, performance-based demonstrations, and competency assessments represent only part, and perhaps not the most important part, of the training process.

The truth is that competency development often intersects with trainees' deep personal feelings and fears: Am I smart enough, confident enough, magnetic enough to be a … supervisor, manager, sales person, leader? Will my performance in this training program be held against me if I make a mistake? What does the group think of me? These emotionally charged, subjective questions involve not just trainees but the trainers themselves, who find their practices framed by human emotions that are typically unaddressed in standard train-the-trainer programs.

Far from being objective, automaton-like beings, trainers are subject to the same human emotions as their trainees. Am I interesting, engaging, knowledgeable? Do my trainees like me? Am I a meaningful trainer? Trainers deal not just with trainees' emotions but also their own. And often those emotions are significant indeed.

The Value of the Meaningful Trainer

Trainers are among the most valuable human resources to their organizations, yet with a few notable exceptions, well-meaning organizational decision-makers tend to promote policies that are at odds with what trainers need and what they actually do. Considering the extent of the resources dedicated to supporting trainers, decisions-makers can make the most of their investment by recognizing what motivates trainers and understanding how to meet their needs effectively. This book will suggest ways in which those who support trainers can do this.

Trainers, for their part, are always seeking ways to do what they do better—to be ever more meaningful to their trainees; and now is the time to introduce the methods that make training more meaningful. Leading thinkers on organizational dynamics have suggested that training in the 21st Century will need to focus not just on the hows of skills and knowledge but also the whys to ensure people know how to learn.

Peter Drucker and Peter Senge have argued that this century's successful enterprises will be "learning organizations" in which every employee is receptive to change and has the ability to think quickly and effectively in response to shifting dynamics. Today more than ever trainers need to find ways to truly impact trainees' way of thinking. This book will show them how to do that.

Key Point 1

21st Century training will need to ensure people know how to learn.

About this Book

The Meaningful Trainer is aimed at trainers and the people who support them. It is based on our 30 years' experience in training—years spent developing training programs, training trainers, writing about training, and leading training. It reflects the real-world experience of people who train every day or on a part-time basis as Subject Matter Expert-trainers. It is about what it means to be a trainer and what trainers mean to the organization. It is designed to help trainers reach the goal of becoming meaningful by suggesting methods that have been proven to enhance the learning process and ensure transfer of learning to the job.   It makes a case for the power of training assessments and sets out practical ways to conduct measurement. It also provides insights for organizational decision-makers that can help ensure trainer satisfaction and retention by focusing on what really matters to this important group.

Overview of the Meaningful Trainer

Chapter One: Becoming a Meaningful Trainer, describes how becoming a trainer is likely to generate a significant transformation in a person. It explains what happens when trainers want to offer more to their organizations as a result of their training experience and how trainers' tend to view their success through the eyes of their trainee.

Chapter Two: Preparing and Supporting Trainers, explains how harnessing the energy and ideas that trainers offer can benefit the organization. It presents best practices around preparing new trainers and supporting incumbents. This is an area in which many organizations fail, often with serious consequences such as trainer disengagement and dissatisfaction.

Chapter Three: The Value of Reflection, describes reflective practice, why it is critical to today's organizations, and how trainers can incorporate it to make their training more meaningful.

Chapter Four: The Meaningful Trainer and the Continuous Improvement Process, explains how trainers have frequently ignored and even undermined the process of evaluating and communicating the business impact of their programs. It describes how to implement continuous improvement for maximum benefit for the trainer and the organization.

Chapter Five: The Meaningful Trainer as a Role Model for the Organization, explains the ways in which the reflective practice model can be leveraged throughout the organization with training leading the effort.

Chapter Six: What it Means to be a Meaningful Trainer, summarizes the ways in which trainers can become more meaningful to the organization.

ONE

BECOMING A MEANINGFUL TRAINER

A Transformative Event

For many, perhaps most trainers, the very act of becoming a trainer is a transformative event. This means that becoming a trainer can cause a fundamental shift in perspective that results in the trainer's becoming, literally, a different person. Transformation is not to be taken lightly. It is a significant experience for anyone who undergoes it, one that can touch all aspects of a person's life.

Jack Mezirow and Stephen Brookfield have done pioneering work on transformative learning. They suggest that a transformation in perspective or a shift in what Peter Senge calls "mental models" occurs along these lines:

1. An event triggers disorientation or a feeling of being in a new place.

2. The event causes the person to examine his or her assumptions.

3. He or she explores ways to resolve the dilemma or simply accepts it.

4. The person develops new perspectives or new ways of thinking.

5. Finally, the person integrates the new way of thinking into his life.

At the center of the transformative experience is a fundamental movement from one way of seeing things to a new point of view. It comes from examining or critically reflecting on previously held assumptions and changing those assumptions to accommodate a new way of thinking.

> Trainers who have positive experiences can make significant contributions to their organization.

For trainers this new way of seeing the world may result in their seeking new opportunities to contribute to the organization; developing a heightened awareness of their own abilities; taking a new interest in continuing education; and a host of other responses.

Most important, trainers who experience a transformation in their way of thinking need support and encouragement from their managers and peers. When they get that support, they can make significant contributions to the organization.

When Training is a Growth Experience

Matt's story illustrates the kinds of changes that can occur when an employee becomes a trainer. Matt is a lead operator at a 300-person manufacturing site who has worked 25 years for the company. Matt served as a Subject Matter Expert to help develop training on new equipment for tenured operators. Six months before we interviewed Matt his manager had asked him to lead a series of training sessions on the new equipment with his work group.

We asked Matt how he was doing in his training assignment. He responded with enthusiasm.

"At first I was worried about whether I could do it. Man, my heart was pounding the first time I led my group. I didn't know how they [the trainees] would accept me. I just figured that not everyone would be happy with what I was doing, but they were! Some of my best trainees saw they could upgrade their skills even if they'd been on the job for years. Two individuals came to me after the first training program and said the program had helped them a lot. That's when I knew I really liked training.

I didn't think this before the training, but now I think that becoming a trainer is a growth experience. See, I've always been nervous in front of a group. My daughter, she has a job in marketing where she has to give presentations all the time. I used to think, 'How can she do that? I couldn't do that.' So when Shelly [his manager] asked me if I wanted to do the training, I said, 'I'd like to but I don't know if I can.' But she said, 'Well, give it a try. I think you'd be good, and I think you really want to do it.' She had faith in me. Even though I was nervous, I wanted to give it a try.

Now it's great. I found out I'm happiest when I'm talking about this job. It's like being a teacher and watching your students change. I think that's interesting, especially at my age—I'm almost 50 years old, you know—to learn something new about yourself and what you can do. And Shelly, she's been behind me 110 percent.

Now that I'm such a quote, 'training expert,' I've gotten my certifications so I can train in bloodborne pathogens and hazard communication. Then the health and safety people asked me to run the CPR training for them. I'm fired up! The whole experience has changed me. My wife sees it and so do my kids. I talk more about everything now to everyone."

We asked Shelly, Matt's manager, whether the changes Matt described had been evident to her.

"Matt's come out of his shell since he started doing this [the training]. I had to persuade him a little at first but that's only because he didn't think he could do it. I knew he could. His confidence now is way, way up. He's training more [subject] areas making a great contribution to the whole site. He's done a real about-face."

New Perspective, New Opportunities

Let's look at what happened to Matt in terms of a transformation in perspective. Initially he was concerned about his ability to train, feeling uncomfortable about his new role. But as the training progressed, he discovered he could do a good job in training. At this point Matt began to reassess his assumptions about his abilities. He started to take on new challenges—challenges he never thought he would seek for himself.

It's important to note that Matt's manager provided him opportunities to grow in new directions, including additional training challenges. When employees undergo a shift in perspective, they are likely to seek innovative ways to apply their enhanced skills and knowledge. Managers who provide trainers with new opportunities to grow leverage trainers' new skills and knowledge for the benefit of the organization and the trainers.

Not all stories are as positive as Matt's. Sometimes—many times—trainers are on their own in dealing with the changes they experience as a result of becoming a trainer. Navigating a transformational experience without support can be a lonely business.

Navigating Change Alone

Here's what Janna, a first-line supervisor, had to say about her experience leading a safety-training program in her company.

"I never liked school or being in a classroom at all. So when we [supervision] were told we'd have to lead this safety program, I thought, 'Oh, no!' But after a few weeks I realized I could do the training pretty well. People said some nice things to me and that felt good. I started to look forward to the training sessions and the on-the-job audits. Then I felt like I was going places. I learned how to speak better, how to handle people better. I started to see how we could do things more safely. I made some suggestions for simple changes and management went along with them. It feels good to see your ideas put into practice.

So after the training program ended, I went to my boss and asked her what else I could do, like maybe leading another

A transformation experience
✓ Challenges assumptions
✓ Creates a dilemma
✓ Results in new perspectives

training program. She looked at me and said, 'You're a supervisor. That's your job.' That was frustrating. I felt like I had more to offer and I could maybe train in other areas, but she didn't care. Now I'm thinking of leaving if I can't find a place to use my training skills in this company."

When Trainers Want to Offer More

Let's look at what happened to Janna and compare her experience to Matt's. Like Matt, Janna wasn't sure she would be a good trainer, but as the training progressed, she discovered she was doing a good job with the program. As she realized she was capable of more than she thought, her perception of herself changed, and she felt she could make a more significant contribution to the company. But when she asked her manager about opportunities to apply her new skills, she was rebuffed. Unlike Matt, who was provided with new challenges, Janna ended up feeling frustrated and possibly looking for a new job.

Employees who become trainers often want to do more, contribute more, be more than what they were before training. They believe they have more to offer their organizations than is commonly recognized. Some trainers succeed in expanding their job roles or taking on new responsibilities; others may leave their organizations to seek opportunities elsewhere. And some simply stay where they are, unhappy and even angry because they know they could do more with their enhanced skills and knowledge.

Key Point 2

Management must be behind the learning process.

What Do They Think of Me?

In many organizations new trainers attend a train-the-trainer session, receive a leader's guide, and are sent on their way to sink or swim. Without ongoing peer or management support, new trainers are left with only one point of reference with regard to their training ability: the trainees. No wonder the deciding factor in whether a new trainer considers a training experience positive or negative has to do with the receptivity of the trainees to the training.

Even the most experienced trainers are likely to consider their trainees' enthusiasm—or lack of it—the most important factor in assessing their success as trainers. Both Matt's and Janna's sense of accomplishment had much to do with the trainees, who responded well to the training.

Key Point 3

Trainers, especially new trainers, tend to judge their performance solely on the basis of their trainees' reactions.

Keep in mind that most trainers are selected because they are experts in their subjects and are willing to share their subject matter expertise. Trainers are often the cream of the crop, and they set high expectations for themselves in any job they do. This can make them hyper-critical of themselves and sensitive to the criticism of others. Trainers are likely to fault themselves when a trainee doesn't acquire skills and knowledge or when a hostile trainee challenges them.

As for the trainees, training can be an unsettling experience. We've said that training often intersects with trainees' feelings of inadequacy or fear of failure, which in turn can cause them to become hostile or disengaged during training. This is what happened to Ravi, an area trainer at a large insurance company.

One Problem Person

Ravi is just completing his first assignment as an area trainer, which means he serves as a trainer in addition to his other job responsibilities. For the past three months Ravi has been training both new and incumbent employees on an innovative customer-relationship model.

Here's what he had to say about the experience.

"I was pretty stoked about being a trainer. I thought it would make my job more interesting. The first people I trained were great, probably because I had a couple of new people who weren't angry and bitter yet. They got the idea behind the CRM [customer-relationship model] and the rest of the folks seemed to go along with them. So that first class was pretty good.

Types of Trainee Resistance

Trainees' resistance to training can come from fear of failure. Trainees show resistance in a variety of ways.

1. Arriving to class late.
2. Disengaging, being quiet, and refusing to participate.
3. Staring at a laptop or cell phone.
4. Talking to other trainees while the trainer is speaking.
5. Trying to monopolize the conversation.
6. Making derogatory comments about the trainer.
7. Continually arguing with the instructor or other trainees.

Then it was time for the next group. Most of those people [in the second group] had been here for at least 10 years. They didn't see my three years' experience [with the company] as very impressive. But most of them were okay, even if they were a little skeptical about what they called the 'fad of the month.' There's a lot of change around here, and some of it doesn't work, so people are kind of skeptical about new things.

I didn't get disheartened until one individual decided she just didn't like me. She pretty much said I didn't know what I was talking about. She would roll her eyes and make little comments to other people in class. It was a miserable experience for me."

Had Ravi tried to talk to the trainee about her resistance? Had he received any training in how to handle difficult situations?

"I didn't really know what to say. I'm not the type of person who gets in your face about things. The only training I had was a one-day train-the-trainer course. We never got into how to deal with someone like this individual."

Still, we pointed out, this was one trainee out of more than 20 participants. Her experience wasn't indicative of that of the entire group.

"Maybe so, but I'm not cut out for a person being sarcastic and rude to me in front of other people for no reason. One problem person just poisoned the whole experience. I'm going to stop being an area trainer and just do my regular job."

One bad experience early on is all it takes to drive some good trainers out of training. Without a support system or means to reassure him that all trainers face this situation, Ravi decided to leave training altogether rather than risk another confrontation.

Key Point 4

Trainers must be provided a meaningful train-the-trainer course to include handling difficult students

Change for Better or Worse

The experience of becoming a trainer is likely to change a person in significant ways. The question is whether the change will be for the better of the person and the organization, or for the worse.

What can organizations do to support their trainers? Certainly a lot more than most of them are doing now. And the fixes aren't expensive. The next chapter suggests how we can prepare and support trainers—and how trainers can prepare themselves—to maximize their value to the organization.

TWO

PREPARING AND SUPPORTING TRAINERS

Harnessing the Energy of Trainers

Encouraging and integrating new ideas are fundamental processes in the learning organization, yet many organizations are missing a critical opportunity to leverage a source of creative energy. This is because they minimize or overlook the significant contributions trainers can make with the enhanced skills and knowledge they develop as a result of becoming trainers. We've seen that becoming a trainer is likely to serve as a catalyst for change. This change can be of significant benefit to the organization if it learns how to tap into it effectively.

How can we support trainers as they grow in their practices? How can we retain trainers and continue to develop them? How can we leverage their enthusiasm for their subject to benefit the larger organization? Some organizations offer best-practice models of how to sustain and develop trainers both for their benefit and the benefit of their organizations. Based on our work with these organizations and our own practices, we offer these recommendations for decision-makers who support trainers.

Start with Great Trainers

In many organizations training was once largely the function of a training department. As the pressure to cut costs continues to build, however, many organizations are turning to in-house subject matter experts to fill at least some training needs. At the same time, many organizations develop employees by placing them on rotational assignments in training. So the training function is frequently populated by people with little or no training experience.

The conventional wisdom is that the "best" employees should become trainers. This is true to an extent, but expertise is only part of the story. There are many things we can teach trainers to help them be successful, but there are some qualities critical to successful trainers that we can't expect to instill in adults if they aren't already there.

What You Can Teach a Trainer	What You Can't Teach a Trainer
✓ Adult learning principles	✓ Enthusiasm for training
✓ The role of learning objectives	✓ Deep knowledge of the subject
✓ Handling disruptions	✓ Interest in people
✓ Presentation skills	✓ Interest in conveying skills and knowledge
✓ Listening skills	✓ Willingness to listen
✓ How to administer tests	✓ Willingness to provide extra help
✓ Treating trainees with respect	✓ Empathy

The most important criterion for a trainer is his or her willingness to do the job. Expertise is important, and lack of expertise is a deal-breaker for a potential trainer. But after that, the person who is doing the training has to want to be a trainer. Peer and supervisor nominations are often a good guide to identifying people with enthusiasm for training.

Many of us can cite cases in which reluctant employees turned into stellar trainers. Those stories are heartwarming, but they're not the norm. In general, forcing a person to be a trainer just because she is an expert in something isn't a good idea. Training demands interaction with people, a positive outlook, and a willingness to listen and provide extra help as needed. Trainers frequently give up their free time to work on lesson plans and provide remediation to struggling learners. It's hard enough to be a good trainer when a person has a desire to do it. It's even more difficult to excel at training when the trainer is reluctant from the outset.

Surprisingly, the best trainers aren't necessarily the most well-educated or

Who Should Train?

Choose trainers who

✓ want to train

✓ like people

✓ are enthusiastic

✓ are nominated by supervisors or peers

✓ have strong job skills

even the fastest learners in a group. Instead, they're the people who had to wrestle a little with learning, the learners who may have figured things out a bit later than others in their class. In fact, very fast learners who become trainers may be impatient with trainees, whereas learners who have had to work at grasping concepts can be more understanding. Provided they have the subject matter expertise and willingness to train, these people tend to show more empathy for learners than those to whom learning comes easily.

Truly Preparing Trainers

Some organizations offer one- or two-day train-the-trainer sessions for new trainers - and some don't even offer that. These programs are fine as far as they go, but they typically don't go far enough to prepare trainers for what might actually happen when they train. Many of these programs provide practice for trainers under nearly ideal conditions. If dealing with hostile or disengaged trainees is included at all, the time devoted to the topic is typically not enough to prepare trainers for what they may encounter in the real world. We've seen train-the-trainer programs that presented problem types of trainees, along with a general discussion about how to address them, with no role-play practice for the trainers.

One objection often raised about providing practice on how to deal with challenging trainees is that it will instill negative ideas in trainers. After all, some trainers may never encounter a problem trainee, so why prepare them for something that may not occur? But most trainers who have been on the job six months have encountered some type of trainee resistance. It may not happen in the first or even the fifth training session, but eventually it will happen.

Remember, trainers are extremely sensitive to trainees' reactions to them. For many trainers the way in which trainees view their efforts is the deciding factor in whether they see training as a positive or negative experience. We owe it to our trainers to prepare them for what they may find on the job. Train-the-trainer sessions should include practice on dealing with trainee resistance. A sample role play at the end of this chapter suggests how to prepare trainers for one type of trainee challenge.

There's another limitation with the standard train-the-trainer program. Considering the kinds of changes in

Key Point 5

All trainers need ongoing support—and this is where organizations most often fail their trainers.

perspective that occur among trainers, train-the-trainer sessions do trainers a disservice by focusing almost exclusively on the objective elements of training. These programs need to take into account the personal and professional changes trainers may experience as a result of becoming a trainer. One company we work with handles this effectively by inviting experienced trainers to talk with trainers at the end of train-the-trainer sessions to describe how becoming a trainer affected them and to take questions from new trainers.

Provide Ongoing Support to Trainers

No matter how robust the train-the-trainer session, it is not enough to sustain trainers indefinitely. Providing support to trainers may seem simple, yet in three decades of working with hundreds of enterprises, we've found very few that do anything in the way of ongoing support for their trainers.

How many good trainers have we lost because their organizations didn't provide mentoring or coaching, leaving them to fend for themselves in unfamiliar territory? Some trainers are lucky enough to have managers who serve as mentors, but many do not have a support system to help them as they develop as trainers.

Ongoing support can be provided in these ways:

- *Mentoring new trainers*—this seems like an easy way to address the challenges new trainers face, but most organizations do not have structured mentoring programs in place. Establishing a mentoring program for new trainers is essential. Mentoring focuses on listening, sharing, and offering guidance to new trainers. It provides a safe space for trainers to surface their concerns and problems. In organizations that offer these programs, trainers have told us that this was a key part of their learning experience.

Mentoring programs offer another important benefit: They provide experienced trainers with a means to apply what they have learned, which helps them contribute more fully to the organization. Most experienced trainers are eager to share what they know, and we need to provide structured opportunities for them to do it. Although savvy new trainers may develop informal mentoring relationships with experienced trainers, we cannot rely on this unstructured approach to developing trainers.

Mentors should be trained in mentoring, not simply assigned mentoring duties. Role-plays in handling sensitive situations and listening for the real issue are key components of learning how to mentor new trainers.

- *Coaching*—unlike mentoring, which is centered on listening and sharing, coaching is focused primarily on developing skills in new trainers. Experienced trainer-coaches observe all or part of a trainer's training session(s) to offer specific guidance into the trainer's practice. Coaching should be as positive as possible within the guidelines of your organizational standards.

- *Learning Journals for Trainers*—both new and experienced trainers benefit from maintaining journals of their training experiences. In fact, this should be part of the new trainer's "curriculum." As we'll see in Chapter Three, reflecting on what has been learned encourages critical thinking around skills and knowledge. This can be difficult for trainers at first, but over time, most find their journals a valuable part of their training.

Ground rules for learning journals include using no names—of trainees, managers, or other trainers—and any other protocols your organization observes for written communications. Trainers can use their journals as springboards for discussion with mentors and as part of their ongoing development during group sessions.

Here is an excerpt from a new trainer's journal.

Barbara's Learning Journal

Today was better than yesterday. Yesterday I wrote that one of the trainees was giving me a problem. He disagreed with me a couple of times about some of the principles of business communications that I was presenting. He said some of the things I was teaching, like writing only with facts, not opinions, were matters of style, and that he should write the way he wants.

I didn't handle that too well I argued back too much and got defensive because I felt like he was picking on me personally. I talked with my mentor, and he reminded me that people can show resistance to change by holding on to what they know. So today I took the trainee aside before class and said that I'd like him to try some of the new things I was suggesting to see how they worked for him. He was very nice about it and said he'd give it a try.

I think he appreciated the extra time I took. Anyway, he was easier to deal with today

---

- *Scheduled group sessions for new and tenured trainers*—these provide support to trainers and can be conducted face-to-face or by virtual technology. Being a trainer places a person in a vulnerable position, one in which she is exposed to personal criticism. When new and tenured trainers are allowed to share challenges, they learn that everyone experiences difficult situations and can discover effective ways of dealing with them.

One training manager told us that his trainers didn't need formal group sessions because trainers had established an "informal network" to support each other. The fact was that some trainers had established an informal support network; others had not, and those that hadn't felt isolated and alienated from the "clique" of trainers who had developed relationships with one another.

Group sessions should be focused and positive while allowing trainers to share legitimate concerns. Ideally they will be action-oriented and solution-based, addressing, and where possible, resolving, issues surfaced during the sessions.

- *A feedback loop*—without a structured feedback loop, trainers can feel disconnected from the organization, and the organization can become disconnected from its trainers. This in turn leads to trainers to believe they are undervalued. Getting out the word to others in the organization about what trainers are doing, what successes they've had, and what issues they've surfaced is routine in some organizations. In others it is not.

Elaine, a savvy management trainer on a rotational assignment, decided to put an end to what she saw as a dangerous disconnect between training and the rest of the company. With her manager's approval, she established a Customer and Stakeholder Advisory Board that met once each quarter to review ongoing and proposed training products and programs. Proposals were evaluated to ensure that programs aligned to overall corporate and departmental objectives; products and programs already in development were assessed to ensure they were meeting the mark in supporting goals. One significant outcome was that several programs that the training department was sure the company supported required extensive modification in goals and objectives to meet stakeholder needs.

During board meetings and through ongoing communication with board members, Elaine alerted customers and stakeholders to key learnings she was gleaning from her experience as a management trainer. The result was real change within the organization based on the stronger connection between training and the board... and in time, a significant promotion for Elaine.

Key Point 6

Trainers and training management should be talking to their customers and stakeholders on an ongoing basis to let them know how training is supporting the goals of the organization.

Provide Opportunities for Trainers to Continue to Develop

Mark has been a trainer with his company for 30 years. Listen to what he has to say about the opportunities he's been provided to develop his skills and knowledge.

"It would be easy to get stale, but [this company] offers a lot of opportunities to learn new things. Over the past three years I've taken workshops in things like advanced principles in teaching adults and constructivism in training.

For me, the best thing they ever did was start a mentoring program where I could work with new trainers.

It's great to help the newbies get over some of those obstacles we all face as trainers."

Mark's company offers unique opportunities for trainer development. But even if an organization can't afford to send its trainers to workshops, it can still provide opportunities for trainers to continue to grow. Developing a mentor program is a relatively low-cost way to recognize experienced trainers and support new ones. And if your organization can't send trainers to classes, ask trainers with special expertise to design a 2- or 4-hour workshop, virtual classroom, or e-learning on a subject of interest for other trainers.

Organizations can also develop internal and external communities of practice. In organizations where trainers are aligned by subject areas, trainers can establish communities to share ideas. These communities can be extended to the entire industry, often through existing professional societies with special interest groups for trainers. Conducting two or three meetings a year involving your trainers and others outside the organization helps trainers cross-pollinate ideas and break free of the "my way/your way" mentality.

A Train-the-Trainer Program

Time Needed: 2 days

Materials Needed: Leader's and Participant's Guides

Day 1:

1. Introduction and overview of the train-the-trainer program.

2. Review of the Leader's and Participant's guides.

3. Introduction to adult learning theory.

4. Discussion: The role of the trainer.

5. Presentation skills:

    - Conducting training in the classroom
    - Using MS PowerPoint
    - Conducting on-the-job equipment demonstrations
    - Encouraging interaction/asking questions
    - Conducting evaluation

6. Preparation and Practice: Trainers prepare and conduct a 5-minute presentation and a 5-minute equipment demonstration from the program. The presentations are videotaped.

7. Individual feedback to the trainers by other trainers and program instructors.

Day 2:

1. Review Day 1.

2. Discussion: Handling challenging trainees.

    - Disengagement

    - Hostility

    - Interruptions

3. Preparation and Practice: Trainees prepare a 5-minute presentation and a 5-minute in-class plant tour. During the presentation one trainee from the group will exhibit challenging behavior based on direction from the instructor.

4. Debrief: What worked, what didn't.

5. The Learning Journal.

6. Final Thoughts/Course Evaluation.

7. Dismiss.

ROLE PLAY

Train the Trainer: The Disengaged Trainee

Trainee:

You are in a training session and checking your phone messages, answering email, and paying no attention to the trainer. You think the training is a waste of time because you already know how to process claims. Supposedly this program has new information, but you doubt it. You are resentful at having to be here and don't mind telling that to the trainer.

Your work is piling up while you're out of the office, and you're using your cell phone to try to keep up with your messages.

Trainer:

This trainee has been checking email and working on his/her cell phone off and on since the session began this morning. You have asked the group to put away laptops and cell phones, but this trainee has ignored you. He/she is becoming a distraction to the class.

Now it's time for a break and you can take the trainee aside. Using the skills you learned in this session, address the trainee and the problem.

Observer:

Did the trainer

8. Use empathetic, probing questions to involve the trainee?

9. Get to the cause of the problem?

10. Show appropriate understanding?

11. Set out the solution?

12. Secure trainee's agreement to implement the solution?

Trainer Coaching Checklist

Did the trainer…

1. Clearly state the objectives of the program?

2. Ask for participants' expectations?

3. Clearly relate the subject matter to the objectives?

4. Clearly state the ground rules for activities?

5. Present the material in a logical, easy-to-follow way as per the Leader's Guide?

6. Answer questions clearly or offer to follow up for more information?

7. Engage the participants in workshops, activities, and discussions?

8. Time activities properly?

9. Summarize material and make transitions clearly?

10. Manage challenging participants?

11. Provide a solid close to the workshop with appropriate follow-up planning?

12. Treat trainees with respect?

13. Recognize areas of misunderstanding and address them?

14. Use materials—journals, job aids, checklists, promotional aids, and so on—in an appropriate way?

15. Your comments to help the trainer:

_____

_____

THREE

THE VALUE OF REFLECTION

Thinking, Feeling, and Learning

Think back to a profound educational or training experience in your life. Take a minute to reflect on it. Then write it down.

_____

_____

Look at what you've written. Is the experience about how much you learned and the skills you acquired, or is it about how surprised, excited, or embarrassed you were by the event?

Most people remember an educational experience because of how it *felt*. What they learned or didn't learn is important, but it's how they felt about the learning that they remember best. And more often than not, the experience is directly related to a teacher or trainer who facilitated the learning. "I never realized I could understand math until my 8th grade teacher made it clear to me. It changed my life," or "That English teacher made me feel terrible," or "I gained so much confidence from that trainer."

Thinking and feeling are inextricably linked in profound learning experiences. Learning often involves an element of emotion, especially when a person believes he has grown in some way from an educational or training experience.

Key Point 7

The meaningful trainer fosters growth among trainees by helping them achieve the skills and knowledge they need to do their jobs effectively.

Fostering Growth: A Key to Meaningful Training

Sometimes during the learning process the trainer is an agent of transformation—that is, during training a trainee may experience a fundamental shift in his way of thinking that permanently changes the way he views the world. For many trainers, even those who train basic skills, fostering this kind of transformation even once in a while is the most satisfying aspect of their jobs.

This was expressed by Davis, who was training case managers in a disability-management company on a new method of interviewing clients.

"I had one trainee who was getting frustrated because she didn't understand why we had this new way [of interviewing]. I asked her to explain how she thought we should do it and when she talked, it came out that she'd never really been trained in her job and didn't know why we do certain things in interviews. And then some other people expressed that they had never been trained either. So I had to take a detour from the lesson plan and get into background that they should have had but didn't.

After the session people came up and thanked me. They said this [the training] had made a huge difference to them. They finally saw why we do things this way. It was a great feeling for me."

Key Point 8

People learn in a variety of ways or styles.

How do People Learn?

The process of learning has been debated by a host of learning theorists, from behaviorists such as B. F. Skinner, who argue that learning is a matter of stimulus -response, to constructivists like J. Bruner, who are mostly concerned with the experiences and contexts that facilitate learning. No one is absolutely certain how people learn, and generalizations on the subject, including those embodied in "adult learning principles," can be contradicted by anyone who doesn't learn in the way that the theorist suggests.

Nonetheless, we have discovered important aspects about the learning process that we can leverage as trainers. For instance, we know that people possess different learning styles, so although not everyone learns by experience, some people do. The meaningful trainer facilitates learning by appealing to different learning styles, providing opportunities for trainees to learn by doing, by listening to short lectures, by participating in discussions, and by seeing visual examples of what is being trained.

Malcolm Knowles's Adult Learning Principles

Malcolm Knowles's called his study of adult learning "andragogy." His principles have been refined as we discover more about learning styles.

1. Adults are autonomous and self-directed.
2. Adults want to leverage their life.
3. Adults are goal-oriented.
4. Adults need to know that what they are learning is relevant.
5. Adults learn by doing.
6. Adults prefer variety in learning.

Yet there are other, deeper ways to reach adult learners that have proven successful and that have yet to be discovered by most trainers. One of the best ways to ensure learners integrate what they learn into their jobs and provide valuable insights to trainers is through what is called reflective practice.

What is Reflective Practice?

Reflective practice, also called critical reflection, involves providing an environment for learners in which they can consider what they are learning in relationship to the assumptions that they hold. It invites learners to challenge preconceived ideas ("I'm not good at writing, I'm better at following than leading, I'm not a good public speaker"). It challenges them to think about what they are learning, how they will apply it, and how it will make a difference in what they do. And it encourages trainees to reflect on the training itself—where it is inspiring them, where they feel comfortable, and where they feel lost. Engaging trainees in critical reflection significantly enhances the trainer's practice by showing him where his assumptions about the training were right or wrong.

Most classroom and on-the-job trainers ask trainees to consider how they will apply what they learned through action plans or "next steps." If we're honest with ourselves, however, we'll acknowledge that even the most sincere action plan is likely to be forgotten as soon as the training is over.

Reflective practice addresses this by encouraging trainees to consider what they are learning, surface their questions and concerns, and in general think about all aspects of learning through a journal that they keep throughout the training. Critical reflection requires both trainers and trainees to surface their preconceived notions and deeply held assumptions about what they're learning so they can integrate new skills and concepts.

As we suggested in Chapter Two, trainers should keep their own journals during training. When critical reflection is a two-way street, it makes training more meaningful for the trainer and the trainee.

Putting Reflective Practice to Use

Let's look at Irene, a full-time sales trainer for a pharmaceutical company, and see how she uses reflective practice to enhance learning in new-hire training, which includes virtual classroom, on-the-job, and e-learning interventions over a six-week period. Her role is to facilitate and manage the virtual classroom sessions, monitor testing, and collaborate with subject matter experts and managers to ensure on-the-job pull-through occurs. Irene discovered the value of critical reflection when she was required to maintain a learning journal for a graduate education course. Since then she's been an enthusiastic advocate of using journals as a means of ensuring critical reflection in training.

Irene tells trainees that they will be keeping journals on what they're learning, the questions they have, and insights they have during the training. She tells them that they'll be required to submit their journals three times, after the second week, after the fourth week, and at the end of their on-the-job-training.

Here are Irene's ground rules for the journals.

DO
1. Think about how what you are learning is affecting you.
✓ What questions do you have?
✓ What concerns do you have?
✓ What is puzzling to you?
✓ What was surprising to you?
✓ What feelings do you have?
2. Reflect on the training that works best for you and why— classroom, on-the-job, or e-learning.
✓ What type of training is most difficult for you?
✓ What does this say about your learning style?
3. What are some things you'd like to learn more about?
4. What is one suggestion you have for the trainer?

DON'T
1. Use the names of trainers or other trainees.
2. Use the journal as a confessional.
3. Be afraid to admit to concerns around learning.

Journals should be respectful but they should also be honest. The best way to ensure honesty is by guaranteeing anonymity. This way you can be certain that you're getting the truth from trainees.

One Trainee's Learning Journal: "Introduction to Pharmaceutical Sales"

I didn't like the training on expense reporting because it was basically a page-turner on a computer. As far as what appeals to me, this isn't it. On the other hand, we had virtual classroom training on regulatory compliance and the instructor was great. I also liked the e-learning on sample accountability. It was very interactive and interesting. I'm not sure what that says about my learning style except that I don't like page-turners.

Getting back to compliance, the instructor had some really good pdfs for us that helped to make the whole compliance thing clearer. I have to admit, though, that I had some questions but didn't ask them because I thought they might be obvious. No one had any questions, so maybe everyone felt the same way, or maybe they understood everything. I'm kind of worried about all the regulations, but the instructor said that our district manager would be reinforcing all of this with us. But it seems like there's a lot to know.

The thing that surprised me the most is how many rules there are. I understand why there all these regulations, but I never knew how complicated they were. Is anyone else feeling overwhelmed by all the rules? Or is it just me?

Cautionary Notes

We have incorporated critical reflection into our practice for over 20 years, and it has significantly enriched the trainees' experience and our own. In short, it has made our training more meaningful. But some cautionary words aimed directly at trainers are in order.

1. No matter how long a person's been a trainer, he'll have to be prepared for some surprises. One of the reasons journals are helpful is that they tell us where we'll need to make corrections, explain further, and address confusion among trainees. Sometimes this information can be delivered in very direct ways. As one of Irene's trainees wrote in her first journal, "I couldn't figure out what you were talking about and I doubt anyone else could, either."

    This is exactly the kind of information we need as trainers, but sometimes it stings. We have to keep in mind that our goal is to improve the training experience—make it more meaningful—and that information like this is just what we need to do it.

2. Since journals may offer some criticism—in fact, it's almost certain that they will, since trainers are fallible human beings—it's important to have a support system in place so trainers can review what trainees say in a dispassionate light. This can be another trainer, a few trainers, or a mentor. The important thing is that this be a safe place where trainers can share trainees' insights without fear of reprisal.

3. The only way to get an honest appraisal of trainers' practice is by ensuring trainee anonymity. This can be a challenge in using e-communications, and trainers may have to receive the journals in hardcopy format. But anonymity is essential to ensuring honesty.

4. Trainers should not start overhauling the entire program based on the first journal entries. Remember that training involves emotions, and some people may be nervous about the program and their performance. We need to achieve a balance between overreacting and being indifferent to what trainees write in early journals. If we've presented a program a number of times and know that it hits the mark, we use the early journals to make minor corrections in the course. If trainees don't see where we're going with something, we note it in our summary and provide an explanation. We don't need to take every comment verbatim and act on it.

Key Point 9

The trainer should be writing a learning journal to surface his concerns, insights, and ideas.

5. Some trainees are not going to like maintaining a journal. The journal requires trainees to reflect on ideas, feelings, and assumptions, and this can be a painful process. And some people just don't like to write. We need to be prepared for at least a bit of complaining, but don't discontinue the journals. Our

experience is that by the end of the session, most if not all trainees agree that the journal was critical to the learning experience.

6. Make sure that reflective practice time is built into all training sessions. Don't expect people to do it as an "extra" before or after training. It's too important for that.

7. Summary and report on the journals after each submission.

Irene's Summary of Trainees' Journals:
Weeks 1-2 of New Hire Training

It seems that everyone liked the presentation on regulatory compliance and that just about everyone is worried about it. It's good to be wary in this area, but I want to reassure all of you that you don't have to know every detail of compliance at the end of the first week. You're going to have lots of reinforcement about this from your district manager and area trainer.

One other thing jumped out of your journals. Most of you are not comfortable asking questions. This reinforces the importance of these journals, but let me remind you that asking questions is a good thing. Don't be afraid to speak up when you have a question. Usually this problem gets better by the third week of training.

Another area of agreement is expense reporting—no one likes the training method. Good news (not for this group, but for future ones) is that we're upgrading this training to be more interactive.

Almost everyone liked the e-learning on sample accountability. Judging by your test results, the training was successful—average score, 95%. And almost all of you are amazed at how much you learned in the first weeks. As one person commented, "I never thought I could get this much new information into my head in 10 days."

FOUR

THE MEANINGFUL TRAINER AND THE CONTINUOUS IMPROVEMENT PROCESS

The Meaningful Trainer Impacts Job Performance

Trainers will agree that training conducted in an organizational setting should be aimed at achieving results that will improve the overall effectiveness of the organization. Trainers may get their reward from the human side of training, but they know what their jobs are all about.

But ask trainers and training management how they know that training is landing on the job, and you're likely to hear responses like these:

- If training weren't doing its job, we'd hear about it from management.

- We don't actually measure it but believe it's doing fine.

- My job is to train skills, not measure performance.
- Our training is very well-received. We don't need to measure it. Everyone agrees it's effective.
- I talk to trainees' supervisors, and they seem to think the training is good.

Except for the last statement, which suggests an attempt to solicit feedback, these answers point to potential trouble for the training organization. They highlight a lack of critical information on the part of trainers and training management that could prove fatal to the training function. In fact, the training director who told us that training was "very well received" at his company was reassigned to a field office shortly after our conversation and his department drastically downsized.

Very few organizations follow up training interventions to learn whether training landed on the job and impacted business results, this is a key to continuous improvement. The result is that training can become disconnected from the rest of the organization in the language it speaks and the metrics it tracks. And this is a dangerous disconnect for training.

Key Point 10

Meaningful trainers want their trainees to apply skills and knowledge on the job.

Working at Cross-Purposes

A customer service sales trainer in a large bank, Keisha has won the highest award the organization can offer a trainer. The award cited her concern for developing people, her high ethical standards, and her contribution to improving the corporate culture. Keisha is dedicated to training, but she has an issue with the new pressure to measure training results.

"Lately it seems like all we talk about is evaluation and job performance and business results. It's all, 'Can you prove that you're improving results?' And we have these meetings and we just go around in circles…how do we measure business impact, are the numbers any good, do we have to do it, how much does it cost, how much time does it take? We have people going to workshops on evaluation and asking all these questions about return-on-investment. And what worries me is that we're losing our focus on people.

Look, I care about performance, of course. But I train in customer service. I just finished a two-day cross-selling program. How do you measure the business impact of that program and prove it changed anything? To me it's too intangible [to measure], and frankly, I don't want to get involved in that stuff. That's not why I got into training. I've talked to Alicia [the branch manager], but she's being pushed by her manager to get into higher level evaluation. I say it's too complicated and not worth it, but no one's listening to me."

A star trainer, Keisha believes no one has taken her concerns into account. Certainly nobody has explained the value of measurement and how it can help Keisha become a more meaningful trainer. So Keisha and organizational decision-makers are working at cross-purposes when both actually want to achieve the same goal—provide meaningful training that improves business results.

Changing What Trainers Do

Trainers are agents of change, but when it comes to changing what *they* do, they are just as suspicious of change as anyone else. Added to this is their legitimate concern that training is undervalued and expendable. This concern is heightened by the reduction in training jobs and outsourcing of training departments over the past decade. In many organizations trainers are nervous, which makes them even more resistant to any change that they feel may further undermine their positions.

This is one reason trainers have been slow to champion a continuous improvement process based on assessments at Levels 3, 4, and 5. What if the evaluations "prove" that their training isn't impacting the business? Could this mean that their programs, and eventually the trainers themselves, will be eliminated?

Another reason trainers may resist higher-level training program evaluation is they don't truly understand how to do it and how it can help them. We've spoken to dozens of trainers and training managers in large, sophisticated companies that had only a vague idea of how to conduct

Level 3, 4, or 5 evaluations or how they could benefit from them. This is unfortunate because done correctly and with trainer involvement, higher-level evaluation can promote the kind of continuous improvement that is key to helping trainers become more meaningful.

Other arguments against higher-level evaluations are that the numbers are unreliable and the cost of such assessments is high. Although these arguments have some truth — in fact, only a percentage of programs should be evaluated at Levels 3, 4, and 5 — trainers should be looking at the programs that invite higher-level evaluation, such as those impacting large number of employees, high-dollar initiatives, product launches, and any programs tied directly to a major corporate objective or initiative.

The High Cost of Resisting Measurement

Ironically, the failure of training to implement a continuous improvement process has placed trainers at higher risk for job loss. The idea that training inhabits a rarified realm that makes it impossible to measure is one of the primary reasons training departments are considered low-hanging fruit by corporate cost-cutters. As Judith Hale points out in Outsourcing Training and Development: Factors for Success (John Wiley & Sons, 2006), page 16.

> When organizations outsource training, they are forced to place a value on it and manage it. They have to decide on deliverables, service levels, and a budget. The organization is then in a better position to monitor expenses.

The flip side of the cost coin is the inability of most training departments to demonstrate that they actually add value through measurable results that impact the bottom line. If value cannot be measured, the basic question that remains is whether it is cheaper to keep the training function in-house or outsource it.

Trainers need to acknowledge that organizations value measurement. Everywhere you look in a typical organization you'll find assessments—of profit and loss, quality and quantity, the cost of goods sold, the impact of marketing. The one area that traditionally has not been measured is training, and training is suffering for it.

The meaningful trainer has to be concerned with whether training lands on the job and leads to improved business results. Trainers should be the people pushing hardest for higher-level evaluations that can tell them what's working, what isn't, and what needs to be modified, yet trainers and training management have engaged in considerable foot-dragging when it comes to measuring results. It's time to stop.

Key Point 11

Trainers should be looking for programs that invite high-level evaluation.

But the Level 1 Assessments Were Great!

Most training organizations conduct Level 1 assessments, known derisively as "smile sheets," to rate customer satisfaction with the training immediately after the training ends. Level 1 evaluations are useful in the context of Level 2, Level 3, and higher evaluations, but in themselves they have limited value.

There are several reasons for this. First, most Level 1 evaluations ask whether the training will be useful on the job, but in many cases it is impossible for trainees to know whether the training will impact their work. This is especially true in new-hire training, where trainees can only speculate about the relevance of the training to their jobs. Second, Level 1 evaluations don't carry much weight with senior leadership. If the best thing we can say about our training is that trainees liked it, we're in trouble.

Kirkpatrick's Levels of Assessment

Level 1—Trainees' reaction immediately after training

Level 2—Test of skills and knowledge

Level 3—Manager's assessment of transfer of learning

Level 4—Dollar value of training

Yet many training organizations rely solely on Level 1 evaluations to make decisions on the efficacy of training. Without the benefit of higher-level evaluations to support Level 1 assessments, leadership is relying on incomplete data to make training decisions.

Putting the Brakes on Assessment

The director of training in a large chain of convenience stores decided that she would conduct Level 3 and 4 evaluations on a long-running classroom training program in handling shrink and spoilage to see whether it was making it a difference to the organization. She told the trainers about her plan at a regular staff meeting.

The three trainers who presented the program immediately raised a number of objections to the plan: Level 1 and 2 evaluations were positive, and evaluations at Levels 3, 4 and 5 would take time and money. Furthermore, they argued, Level 3, 4, and 5 data are unreliable, and it would be "impossible" to capture dollar values accurately.

Later discussions with these trainers suggested that their real objections (unacknowledged even to themselves) arose from their concern that the program might not prove to have made a significant difference to the company, even though they were sure it had enhanced trainees' skills in reducing shrink and spoilage. They saw the evaluation plan as a not-so-subtle means of placing their program in a negative light so that it could be dropped as part of a corporate cost-cutting scheme. Nothing could have been further from the truth, but in the end the trainers' opposition proved impossible to overcome, and the idea was dropped entirely for six months.

Doing Assessment the Right Way

But the director of training was persistent. She realized that her initial approach had been threatening to the trainers, and she decided to try again with a new strategy. This time she asked the trainers to collaborate with her on the evaluation plan. She acknowledged the power of the Level 1 and 2 assessments and explained that evaluation at Levels 3 and 4 could make the lower-level assessments even more meaningful. She explained that she wanted trainers to work with her on the evaluation plan before the next course implementation so they could suggest appropriate metrics based on their deep knowledge of the subject.

With trainers cautiously on board, they realized as they discussed post-training evaluation that the program had a weakness—that is, there was no on-the-job intervention to pull through the training. Studies suggest that 75- 80% of classroom is forgotten within two weeks if it isn't reinforced on the job. Realizing that a lack of post-classroom intervention would have a negative impact on higher-level assessments, one of the trainers developed on-the-job interventions for store supervisors and managers to ensure training landed on the job. This alone made the training more meaningful.

Then the trainers set about conducting Level 3 evaluations, asking store supervisors about the value of the training. Results were almost universally positive. "I saw shrink and spoilage decrease by 10% after the training" was a common response.

Finally, trainers put dollar amounts to pre- and post-program shrink and spoilage numbers. The results were that a training program that cost about $35,000 a session (based on managers' time out of store, hotel, meals, trainer and transportation costs) yielded over $60,000 in savings from reduced shrink and spoilage.

Key Point 12

80% of classroom training is lost within two weeks of training if it's not reinforced on the job.

The Importance of Pulling Through Training

As the trainers in the convenience store chain discovered, one way to reduce their anxiety about assessment is by ensuring that programs contain on-the-job pull-through of training. The meaningful trainer wants to make sure that her training truly makes a difference to the trainee and the organization. This means she needs to develop interventions that ensure training lands on the job and impacts the business.

One objection raised to on-the-job interventions is that they typically involve the trainee's manager or supervisor. Yet the best training organizations recognize that management involvement is critical to maximizing the impact of training. And just one trainer can make a significant difference in a culture that doesn't typically include management support for training.

This is what happened when Jamal, a training manager at a retail organization, realized that a classroom program in negotiation skills training for buyers needed on-the-job pull-through.

"We saw that if training were to be successful it would have to be aimed directly at the real-world situations buyers faced. The classroom training conducted by a vendor for a variety of companies is good, but it isn't job-specific. We also saw we needed to include customer accountability for ensuring business results. Buyers' managers would have to commit to pulling through key concepts and showing value for what was taught. This in turn meant that managers would have to learn what was presented in the training program and reinforce key skills and concepts on the job. So in the end we decided to see whether we were making an impact by evaluating the program through Level 4, which focuses on dollar results."

Jamal summed up the challenges this way:

- How would the training department, along with buyers and managers, establish metrics to evaluate business impact?

- How would training secure managers' commitment to participate?

- What kinds of activities would training need to develop to ensure pull through?

- How to overcome the idea that soft skills can't be evaluated?

- Would evaluation constitute a significant investment in time and money?

Implementing the Pull-Through and Evaluation Plan

Jamal's efforts to implement the assessment plan were significant. The company had never integrated learning in the way he was proposing, and he had some resistance to overcome along the way.

First, Jamal called each buyer who planned to attend the program and his or manager to describe the course, its learning objectives, on-the-job requirements, and expected business outcomes. Then he explained that managers needed to take part in a pre-course assessment of negotiations skills and send in those assessments six weeks before classroom training. Participation in the program depended on completing this assessment. Jamal also asked managers to suggest metrics to assess the business impact of the program.

At the six-week deadline Jamal had received exactly one pre-course assessment out of the 14 he was expecting. At this point it became clear that securing manager involvement would take more effort. With the support of the director of training, Jamal conducted a 45-minute online meeting to introduce managers to the content of the program and their responsibilities in it. He secured their commitment to complete the pre-course assessments by the end of that week. He also got agreement on the metrics to be assessed, which were centered on evaluating specific contracts before and after training to measure changes in dollar values.

Once the pre-course assessments were completed, buyers attended the classroom training. Then they participated in on-the-job training activities that Jamal had developed in the form of a field activity guide. The activities involved skill application on the job and role-play with the manager over the course of four weeks. Jamal sent two emails to buyers and managers reminding them that certification in the program depended on completing the on-the-job activities and final assessment, as well as the business impact evaluation.

"It was a challenge to get people on board with this because we were changing the entire culture around training," Jamal says. "When something is new you have to work a little harder. In our Level 4 evaluations we asked managers to place a value on the increase in negotiation skills. With a confidence level of 75%, managers reported buyers were doing business a lot better based on a review of contracts. Here's what one manager said: 'I have found a huge benefit from the course. [Negotiation] is a core competency that makes a big difference. We have saved millions of dollars already.' "

Thanks to Jamal's efforts in evaluation, management is now playing the part it should play in training and is recognizing the benefits of training in improving business results.

The Value of Assessment

Training for sales personnel at a large investment company typically involved a two-week, on-site onboarding experience at corporate headquarters. Recently management decided to move new-hire training entirely off-site, eliminating all classroom training. Training would now be conducted at the trainees' field offices through virtual classroom, e-learning, and on-the-job interventions.

Before implementing the plan, training management developed an evaluation strategy based on measuring the most recent new hires' selling metrics at three- and six-months post-training. Then they would compare those metrics with those of the last classroom-trained group. Since sales metrics were already being tracked, it made sense to use them as a means of comparison.

The training was moved off-site and the evaluation took place as planned. When management compared the selling metrics of the last group trained in the classroom against those of the first group trained off site, they found they had increased one-half of a percentage point in the new group, translating into hundreds of thousands of dollars in revenue for the company. This more than offset the cost encountered in moving the training offsite – and it gave the training department an important win that it could communicate throughout the company.

Key Point 13

*Training departments must be aware of and
responsible for their costs.*

In addition, the training department saved significantly on travel, meal, and lodging costs for participants. Training departments that are aware of and responsible for costs associated with travel are incorporating more distance options in their curricula. Continuous improvement is critical to making the most of resources in all organizations.

How Reliable are the Numbers?

Whenever the subject of higher-level assessment comes up, someone is certain to challenge the reliability of the evaluation. Here are the most common arguments made against higher-level assessment:

- You can't measure the impact of soft-skill training.

- Training is just one part of the equation. How do we separate it from other things we're doing, like marketing and advertising?

- No one is going to believe the numbers.

In fact, we *can* measure the impact of soft-skill training, as the negotiation skills example suggests. The challenge lies in establishing metrics and assessing them pre- and post-training. Training departments that consistently measure business impact and can show a correlation with improved business results over time develop a powerful story that supports the training effort.

The issue of teasing out the impact of training from other interventions also comes up frequently. Like marketing, advertising, and learning from primary school on, training isn't conducted in a sterile environment. The threat of "contamination" from things other than the independent variable—in this case, training—is always with us. If training is conducted in conjunction with other major initiatives, such as installing new equipment or launching a major marketing campaign, the impact of training can be weighted as a percentage of the entire initiative. If the metrics are agreed upon in advance and the evaluation strategy is approved before the training, customers and stakeholders will be more likely to accept the numbers.

In any case the metrics used to assess training impact should be those valued by the customers and stakeholders— not, as too often happens, those valued only by the training department, such as how many people were trained or how many rated the program "very helpful" on a Level 1 evaluation. These metrics mean little to those outside the training organization. Training should be measured by what is valued by its customers.

Key Point 14

Metrics should be those valued by customers and stakeholders.

The Power of the Testimonial

Training typically doesn't tout its successes—and too often, it isn't even aware of them. One of the most powerful ways to measure the business impact of training, keep in touch with customers, and broadcast training success is by leveraging testimonials from influential decision-makers within the organization.

Level 3 evaluations are an ideal way to do this. Level 3 data are based on managers' or supervisors' assessments of trainees' performance. These evaluations place trainers in front of their customers and yield important information about customers' perceptions of training success. Conducting Level 3 evaluations, especially by personal interviews or telephone, helps ensure training is meaningful to the organization.

Conducting Level 3 evaluations on key training programs encourages managers to reflect on the value of training to their employees. We've seen the value of critical reflection in developing trainees and trainers; the same is true with managers. And when an influential manager or thought-leader endorses a training intervention, trainers should think about leveraging that endorsement as a part of a communication strategy that keeps customers and stakeholders in the loop and keeps training in the forefront of the organization.

Level 3 Assessment
Safety Training
Supervisor Questionnaire

Over the past 3 months we have been conducting safety training for shop-floor employees and supervisors. Have you…

1. seen a reduction in lost workday cases?
2. noticed that employees are conducting more safety audits?
3. noticed that employees are talking about safety?
4. seen employees behave more safely – for instance, wearing proper PPE?
5. comments?

Our experience has shown that nothing is more effective in establishing the value of training than testimonials from high-visibility people who can speak to training impact. As you might expect, the most convincing testimonials are combined with data. "My department experienced a reduction in defects..." or, "We had a sales increase of..." Almost any training organization can gather information on the success of training from learners, their managers, and stakeholders.

Communicating Results

One of the biggest mistakes training departments make is to assume that the organization knows and values what it does. In some organizations this is true. In many it is not. This is evident in the resentment we've heard managers express when their employees are "out" at a training session, not to mention the hostility voiced by some trainees at having to attend training. Training needs to do more to communicate its value to its customers and stakeholders.

Communication doesn't have to include charts, graphs, and statistics. A short email blast sharing results from a recent training program or endorsements from high-profile stakeholders is enough. When communication is consistent, easy to understand, and targeted, stakeholders take notice and training begins to achieve high marks in the organization.

Great Results for ASR Training —
and You Made it Happen! (Flash email)

Thanks to all who participated in ASR training (Achieving Sales Results) as a participant or a coach. We've just completed Level 3 evaluations to learn how managers assessed the program, and the results are excellent. Out of the 30 managers surveyed, 28 tell us that they've seen significant improvement in their sales reps' closing skills and most important, an increase in sales in their territories.

Here's what manager Jean Romero had to say: "This program really hit the mark. Many of my people have improved their sales, one by 5%! I highly recommend this program to my peers."

We look forward to continuing to work with you on this important program.

FIVE

THE MEANINGFUL TRAINER AS A ROLE MODEL FOR THE ORGANIZATION

The Meaningful Trainer and Organizational Leadership

Once a reflective practice model is in place in the training organization, it can be extended with good result to any group, especially those new to management and the senior executive suite. This is one way to facilitate the learning organization and eventually enhance the skills and knowledge of all employees.

Why do new managers and senior executives need this kind of intervention? Here's what Evelyn, a new assistant vice president in a healthcare organization, had to say.

"You know who really needs training in this company? People like me. Of course, no one will say it, but it's true. There's an assumption that because you've reached this level you know how to do things, but there is a lot I have to feel my way through. If we had some kind of training for senior leadership, I could save a lot of time. I feel like I'm slogging through mud here, trying to figure out what I'm doing. But I wouldn't dare say that to anyone.

A lot of times I feel anxious and uncertain about what I'm doing. I think I'm spending time worrying about things that could have been addressed in training or even in a mentoring program. This whole transition could have been a lot smoother. And I'll bet a lot of other people feel the same way."

When Training Needs Go Unnoticed

One consequence of letting training needs go unaddressed is that people like Evelyn become anxious about what they don't know. This takes valuable energy away from getting things done and tamps down creativity. As a recent study showed, employees who are dissatisfied for any reason—for example, because they feel uncertain and sometimes frustrated—have less energy available for creating value propositions for customers.

Customer Satisfaction Begins with the Employee

Employee satisfaction leads to
→ Value creation, which leads to
→ Customer satisfaction, which over time leads to
→ Customer loyalty, a hallmark of the highly satisfied customer, and
→ Profit and growth.

(The GE Leadership Effectiveness Survey, 2009)

A Model for Organizational Change

Just as we use a reflective practice model for trainers, we can implement the same model with any employee, no matter where he is in the organizational hierarchy. Ideally, every employee will have training in his or her job, but practically, the further up we go in the organization, the less likely it is that an employee will be exposed to formal training opportunities targeted specifically to his job.

But aren't employees at the higher levels of the organization able to figure things on their own? Yes, most do eventually. Yet think of the time wasted and energy expended in reaching peak performance—time that could have been saved by training or at least mentoring the employee.

In fact, many successful senior managers have developed informal mentoring relationships with a trusted confidant within or outside of their organizations. Here's what Patrick, an executive at a mid-sized manufacturing company, said about the person who became his mentor as he rose through his organization.

"Laurence [a manager] and I developed a close friendship after he hired me as a level 1 engineer. He seemed to take a special interest in me and made himself available to listen to my concerns and answer my questions. I was really brand new—this was my first job out of college and I was pretty unsure of myself. I wouldn't have been as successful as I was if Laurence hadn't helped me.

After a couple of years Laurence moved on to another company, but we stayed in touch. When I got promoted to manager, he and I talked a lot. He gave me tips and I told him my problems. He helped me understand that my nervousness was part of the job and the challenges I was facing were normal. He gave me the confidence I needed to take action.

Over the years I got more promotions and Laurence was always my sounding board. He's retired now but we still talk.

Key Point 15

Employees promoted without a training curriculum or developmental pathways are most at risk for being isolated and focused on their concerns.

What I'd wish for people coming up through the company is that they don't have to learn by trial and error. We need a pathway for people that recognizes that folks at every level need to be developed. Lately I've been thinking that maybe I could help someone the way Laurence helped me because he made a big difference to my career."

Training departments can lead the way in implementing reflective practice in their organizations at all levels by promoting the same kinds of mentoring, group support, and reflective practice that they use for trainers. As we've learned from working with trainers, implementing a reflective-practice model can help senior-level employees navigate through change with successful outcomes.

Mentor's Guide to Mentoring Activity for Regional Director: What is the Financial Condition of Your Region?

Time Needed

30 minutes

Objectives

- Align strategy to financials

- Address any fear of dealing with numbers

- Create clarity that allows the non-financial profession to understand financials in order to take actions to drive results

Rationale and Activities

- Present the value proposition

- Align the value proposition to financials

- Discuss financial tools
  - Trended analysis
  - Forecasting

Resources

- Financial reports for latest quarter in the region

- List of References provided at the end of this guide

The Human Potential

As we said at the beginning, at the heart of being a meaningful trainer is the recognition that no enterprise can thrive if its employees do not grow—both in themselves and in their jobs. Trainers who can help employees understand the significance of what they bring to the organization—and can help the organization understand the significance of its employees—are truly meaningful trainers.

SIX

WHAT IT MEANS TO BE A
MEANINGFUL TRAINER

Acknowledging the Value of Trainers

As the group charged with transmitting organizational knowledge and culture to employees, trainers should be considered valuable human resources, but often this is not the case. Many trainers are expected to do new jobs without anything approaching adequate trainer training and support. We fail our trainers when we don't provide them the resources and experiences they need to be successful. And we disable the organization as a whole when we don't capitalize on the contribution trainers can make.

We started by saying that trainers train to make a difference and that the human side of training is important to them. In fact, left to their own devices, trainers will regard trainees' reactions to training as the sole barometer of their efficacy as trainers; even one disgruntled trainee can de-rail a good trainer if she doesn't have the support of a mentor or other experienced trainers. As agents of change, trainers are likely to encounter resistance as well as enthusiasm when they challenge trainees, and emotions frequently surface during the training process. Yet it's the human side of training that we frequently ignore when we prepare our trainers.

It Changed my Life

For many trainers the very process of becoming a trainer may be a transformative event. All the more reason to provide them support in the form of robust train-the-trainer sessions, mentoring, coaching, reflective practice, and new opportunities to grow. In short, the transformation that often occurs among employees-turned-trainers needs to be acknowledged and encouraged. When it is not encouraged, trainers may experience dissatisfaction with the organization.

The Reflective Practice

Remember that most people recall key educational or training experiences because of how those experiences felt, and thinking and feeling are inseparably linked in profound learning experiences. Reflective practice acknowledges the feeling around in learning while focusing on the growth that takes place during the learning experience. It also helps prepare learners to think critically about what they are learning - and critical thinking is a key element for success in the 21st Century work environment.

For trainers reflective practice can take the form of a journal in which they share their experiences with mentors or managers. For trainees learning journals will include their reflections on what they are learning and their reactions to it. Once a reflective practice model is in place in the training organization, it can be extended with good result to any group, especially those new to management and the senior executive suite. This is one way to facilitate the learning organization and eventually enhance the skills and knowledge of all employees.

The Power of Assessment

One area in which trainers have tended to put on the brakes is in championing a strong continuous improvement process that incorporates higher-level assessment and a robust communication plan. This has actually made trainers more vulnerable to the charge that at least some training is simply "nice to have" and not essential to a thriving organization.

Assessment does not have to be a complicated affair. Indeed, one of the most powerful ways to assess the business impact of training, get to know training customers, and highlight training success is by gathering testimonials from influential leadership in Level 3 evaluations. Talking with the people who manage our trainees is essential to understanding their needs, their perceptions, and their real view of training. Yet very few training organizations maintain strong ties with their customers. No wonder, then, that these same customers are likely to question the value of training when it comes time to cut costs.

The meaningful trainer has to be concerned with ensuring training leads to measurable, improved business results. Rather than resisting higher-level evaluation, trainers should be leading the charge to find out what's working for the enterprise and what isn't. Higher-level assessment can generate important changes in the efficacy of training. For example, classroom trainers who are faced with assessment of business results may realize that to be effective, classroom training needs to be augmented with on-the-job pull-through. This kind of information is vital to the meaningful trainer.

Summary

Trainers who transmit skills and knowledge to employees are critical to the organization, and we owe it to our trainers to provide an environment that will enhance their success. And trainers owe themselves and their organizations tangible assessments of training effectiveness. The 21st Century challenges for trainers and their organizations call for an approach to training and training effectiveness that addresses the human side of training while delivering sound business results. This is the province of the meaningful trainer.

CONCLUSON

KEY POINT SUMMARY

1. 21st Century training will need to ensure people know how to learn.

2. Management must be behind the learning process.

3. Trainers, especially new trainers, tend to judge their performance solely on the basis of their trainees' reactions.

4. Trainers must be provided a meaningful train-the-trainer course to include handling difficult students.

5. All trainers need ongoing support—and this is where organizations most often fail their trainers.

6. Trainers and training management should be talking to their customers and stakeholders on an ongoing basis

to let them know how training is supporting the goals of the organization.

7. The meaningful trainer fosters growth among trainees by helping them achieve the skills and knowledge they need to do their jobs effectively.

8. People learn in a variety of ways or styles.

9. The trainer should be writing a learning journal to surface his concerns, insights, and ideas.

10. Meaningful trainers want their trainees to apply skills and knowledge on the job.

11. Trainers should be looking for programs that invite high-level evaluation.

12. 80% of classroom training is lost within two weeks of training if it's not reinforced on the job.

13. Training departments must be aware of and responsible for their costs.

14. Metrics should be those valued by customers and stakeholders.

15. Employees promoted without a training curriculum or developmental pathways are most at risk for being isolated and focused on their concerns.

APPENDICES

Appendix 1
Trainer Survey

This is the survey we used with the trainers that served as a starting point for interviews.

Date

Dear _____:

Recently you participated in a training program serving as a trainer. We are doing research on the kinds of changes that may occur as a result of taking part in this kind of activity. Now we are asking for your help in this research project.

This project has two parts: The first is a short survey (enclosed) that you can complete in about 15 minutes; the second is a one-hour interview that we can conduct during your lunch hour – or, at your convenience.

The survey is confidential and will not be disclosed unless you allow it. It includes a section for your name, extension, and best time to call you. We would appreciate your returning it in the envelope provided by _____.

I look forward to receiving your survey and meeting with you.

Survey

1. Think back to when you were first asked to be a trainer. Which of the words below best describe your reaction when you were asked to be a trainer? (Check one)

    ☐ Very enthusiastic

    ☐ Somewhat enthusiastic

    ☐ Did not care

    ☐ Somewhat reluctant

    ☐ Very reluctant

2. Which of the words below best describes how you felt when you led your first training session: (Check one)

    ☐ Very enthusiastic

    ☐ Somewhat enthusiastic

    ☐ Did not care

    ☐ Somewhat reluctant

    ☐ Very reluctant

3. Please describe how you feel now about leading training.

4. If your feelings have changed about leading training, describe what factors you think caused the change.

5. Which of the words below best describes your level of job satisfaction <u>before</u> you began leading the training?

    ☐ Very satisfied

    ☐ Somewhat satisfied

    ☐ Neither satisfied nor dissatisfied

    ☐ Somewhat dissatisfied

    ☐ Very dissatisfied

6. How do you feel now about your job?

    ☐ Very satisfied

    ☐ Somewhat satisfied

    ☐ Neither satisfied nor dissatisfied

    ☐ Somewhat dissatisfied

    ☐ Very dissatisfied

7. If your feelings towards your job have changed, describe the factor(s) that caused the change.

8. Which of the words below best describes your level of satisfaction with your co-workers <u>before</u> you began leading the training?

    ☐ Very satisfied

    ☐ Somewhat satisfied

    ☐ Neither satisfied nor dissatisfied

    ☐ Somewhat dissatisfied

    ☐ Very dissatisfied

9. How do you feel now about your co-workers?

    ☐ Very satisfied

    ☐ Somewhat satisfied

    ☐ Neither satisfied nor dissatisfied

    ☐ Somewhat dissatisfied

    ☐ Very dissatisfied

10. If your feelings towards your co-workers have changed, describe the factor(s) that caused the change.

11. Can you think of an incident that occurred during the training that most impressed or affected you in any way?

12. Do you have any comments about any changes that might have occurred in other areas of your life related to your role as a trainer?

The second part of this research involves a follow-up an interview. Please write your name and extension below so we can call you to arrange a time to speak with you.

Name: _____

Phone/Extension: _____

Best times to call: _____

Appendix 2
Measuring Training Effectiveness Sample

Level	What is Measured	How to Measure
Level 1 - Reaction	How participants perceive a program's content, design, and delivery. This is basically an immediate measure of "participant satisfaction."	Questionnaires (Evaluation Forms) completed by participants at training program conclusion. XYZ uses a standard "Global Education and Training Course/ Instructor Evaluation Form." The scores from this form can be compiled and analyzed to determine trends and make improvements. An overall score of 4.2 out of 5.0 is the XYZ global standard for course and instructor evaluations.
Level 2 - Learning	Whether knowledge was acquired, skills improved, or attitudes changed due to training. Here, you measure if participants learned what you intended them to learn.	• Observed simulations, skill demonstrations, application exercises, role plays, etc. • Can include pre- and post-tests

Level	What is Measured	How to Measure
Level 3 – On-the-Job Application	Whether participants are using what they learned on the job. This is a measure of the extent to which participants change their on-the-job behavior due to training.	• Job performance observations • Interviews and/or post-training surveys with trainees and their managers
Level 4 - Impact on Business Results	The impact of the training investment. This requires a baseline of items to be measured before the training. This is a measure of the business results that occur due to training. Could include increased sales, higher productivity, bigger profits, reduced cost, streamlined work processes, greater customer satisfaction, improved employee climate.	• Cost-benefit analysis • Tracking operational results • Interviews with Senior Management on business results

Level	What is Measured	How to Measure
Level 5 - Return on Investment (ROI)	The ROI is based on establishing baseline measures before training and assigning costs to each area to be measured. All costs associated with the training are gathered. 3 to 6 months after the training, reductions in costs of the items to be tracked are measured against the cost of the training to establish ROI.	• Establish costs of selected items before training • Establish all costs associated with training • Track costs of selected items 3–6 months after training • Establish ROI

Appendix 3
Overview of Training Measurement:
The 5 Levels

Levels of Evaluation

Donald Kirkpatrick specified 4 levels of evaluation--reaction, learning, application, and impact on the business. Recently a new and important level has been added, Level 5, which measures Return on Investment (ROI) in training.

Although in the past most training evaluations typically ended at Level 2, more and more trainers are finding that they must evaluate training results in ways that will convince the business to invest in training. This is why all levels of evaluation are important.

Level 1

Level 1 evaluation measures trainees' reactions to the training. This evaluation is often administered through the well-known "smile sheet," a survey or questionnaire distributed immediately after the training. Level 1 evaluation assesses whether trainees thought the training met its objectives, whether the instructor presented the material effectively, and whether the training will affect their performance on the job.

Level 1 evaluation is important because it tells us whether or not we met our trainees' expectations for the program. Even the best-designed training program will not be effective if trainees find it boring, confusing, or disorganized. This level of evaluation is important because we need to know whether we are meeting trainees' demands for training. Level 1 tells us whether and where we need to make modifications in the program for user acceptance.

For years many organizations evaluated only Level 1. Even though it is important to know how trainees reacted to the training, Level 1 is far from the whole story. We should not rely solely on Level 1 reactions to make determinations about which training is successful and which is not.

Level 1 evaluation is relatively easy to administer and analyze. Many organizations have a 100% target for Level 1 evaluation to ensure all programs have this level of assessment.

Level 2

Level 2 assessments tell us whether learning or skill development occurred as a result of the training Typically measured by a pre- and post-test, Level 2 shows the extent to which trainees grew in knowledge or skill during the training. Level 2 is critical to deciding whether training is meeting the mark set by the objectives.

Testing before and after training tells what trainees knew when they arrived at the program and what they learned during the training; and post-test results tells us where modifications need to be made to improve knowledge or skill transfer. Suppose, for instance, that trainees consistently missed a certain question on the post-test. That tells us that this area of the program or the post-test itself needs to be improved.

Training should always include a pre- and post-test of some kind, through demonstration, written evaluation, or other form. These evaluations can be conducted before and after training in the classroom, job site, or wherever the training occurred. Level 2 evaluation should occur in 100% of training.

Level 3

Level 3 evaluation takes place when trainees return to the job. It measures whether new learning or new skills are actually demonstrated in the job setting. For example, suppose trainees participated in a program designed to develop leadership skills. Level 3 measurements might include a survey of trainees' supervisors or managers to learn whether trainees demonstrated leadership qualities on the job. It might also include trainees' peers and subordinates to learn their perceptions of trainees' new leadership skills.

Similarly, a training program aimed at improving maintenance mechanics' troubleshooting skills might involve a survey of mechanics' supervisors or team leaders to learn whether trainees' competencies in troubleshooting skills improved. It might also involve a review of maintenance records and equipment downtime conducted after the training to learn whether new skills were being demonstrated on the job.

Level 3 evaluations are more time-consuming and more dependent on feedback after the training ends than are Levels 1 and 2. Many organizations set a target of 40 to 50% for Level 3 evaluations.

Level 4

Level 4 evaluations are concerned with the impact of training on the business. For example, a Level 4 evaluation of a training program designed to reduce errors in drug tableting would focus on the number of errors recorded before and after the training to see whether errors dropped after the program. A training program focused on increasing sales would measure sales results before and after training.

One reason trainers have been reluctant to evaluate business results is the concern that intervening variables may affect outcomes. Suppose, for instance, that a new tableting method is introduced after the training and errors in tableting increase. Or suppose a competitive product comes on the market, reducing sales of the product that was trained. How do we account for these variables?

The answer is to know the environment before and after the training, correcting for variables as necessary in the Level 4 evaluation. This is why it is important to collect data before the training occurs on error rates, quality issues, sales data, and so on. The more extensive and tangible your baseline data, the better able you are to show what Level 4 results were and what might have affected them.

Level 4 evaluations require a baseline of information before and after the training. Because these evaluations can be time-consuming and difficult to conduct, organizations may set targets of 10 to 20% for Level 4 assessments.

Level 5

Level 5 evaluation measures ROI by comparing the costs of training with the benefits of the program. Although this level of evaluation is still relatively rare, it is becoming more and more important in the training community because training managers and program developers are now being asked to prove their value to the organization.

Jack Phillips has noted that Level 5 evaluation works with all the other levels to measure the overall affect of the program. Including the other levels is critical in assessing the training because each level provides a snapshot of reactions or results at various points along the training continuum. No single level provides a complete picture of the success of the training. Because it is a time-consuming process, Level 5 evaluation may occur in only 5% of training program evaluation.

One argument sometimes made against ROI is that "training results can't be measured." This assumes that training is too intangible in its affect to be reduced to quantitative assessments. But the fact is that training results can be measured in quantitative terms, provided the baseline measures are established at the beginning of the training. This is the case with any measure of ROI, including investment in new facilities, equipment, or modifications to the plant.

For Further Reading

1. *Establish a Business Case for Training.* ASTD Infoline. Volume 24, Issue 0709, September, 2007. (Domenick, Gallup, Gillis)
2. Hale, Judith. *Outsourcing Training & Development: Factors for Success.* Pfeiffer, 2006.
3. Kirkpatrick, Donald and James. *Evaluating Training Programs: The Four Levels.* Berrett-Koehler, 2006.
4. Phillips, Jack J. and Stone, Ron Drew. *How to Measure Training Results: A Practical Guide to Tracking Six Key Indicators.* McGraw-Hill, 2002.

ABOUT THE AUTHORS

Kate Domenick, Ed.D., has served as a principal and managing partner of the Training and Communications Group, Inc. since 1982. In that capacity she has worked with hundreds of trainers, managing projects that involve designing, producing and evaluating training programs and preparing trainers to design and deliver training.

David A. Gallup, Ed.D., has served as a principal and managing partner of the Training and Communications Group, Inc. since 1982. He established and served as the first advisor to Penn State's Graduate Program in Instructional Systems Design for its Great Valley campus. He has consulted in training services to over 100 Fortune 500 firms in training and development.